BASIC DEVELOPM
SCREENING: 0–4

The Normal Child, 8th edition, 1982
Churchill Livingstone, Edinburgh
Translated into Greek, Spanish, Japanese, French and Farsi

*The Development of the Infant and Young Child, Normal
and Abnormal*, 7th edition, 1980
Churchill Livingstone, Edinburgh
Translated into Japanese, French and Polish

*Lessons from Childhood: Some Aspects of the Early Life of
Unusual Men and Women* with
C. M. Illingworth, 1968,
Churchill Livingstone, Edinburgh
Translated into Japanese

Babies and Young Children: Feeding, Management and Care
with C. M. Illingworth
6th edition, 1977
Churchill Livingstone, Edinburgh

*Treatment of the Child at Home: A Guide for Family
Doctors*, 1971
Blackwell Scientific Publications, Oxford
Translated into Greek

Common Symptoms of Disease in Children
8th edition 1984
Blackwell Scientific Publications, Oxford
Translated into Spanish, Greek and Italian

The Child at School: A Paediatrician's Manual for Teachers, 1975
Blackwell Scientific Publications, Oxford

Your Child's Development in the First Five Years, 1981
Churchill Livingstone, Edinburgh

Infections and Immunization of your Child, 1981
Churchill Livingstone, Edinburgh

Basic Developmental Screening: 0–4 years

RONALD S. ILLINGWORTH

MD (Leeds), Hon MD (Sheffield), FRCP (Lond), DPH, DCH
Emeritus Professor of Child Health,
The University of Sheffield
Formerly Paediatrician to the
Children's Hospital and Paediatrician to the
Jessop Hospital for Women
The United Sheffield Hospitals

THIRD EDITION

BLACKWELL SCIENTIFIC PUBLICATIONS

OXFORD   LONDON   EDINBURGH
BOSTON   PALO ALTO   MELBOURNE

© 1973, 1977, 1982 by Blackwell Scientific Publications
Editorial offices:
Osney Mead, Oxford, OX2 0EL
8 John Street, London, WC1N 2ES
23 Ainslie Place, Edinburgh, EH3 6AJ
52 Beacon Street, Boston, Massachusetts 02108, USA
667 Lytton Avenue, Palo Alto, California 94301, USA
107 Barry Street, Carlton, Victoria 3053, Australia

DISTRIBUTORS

USA
  Year Book Medical Publishers
  35 East Wacker Drive
  Chicago, Illinois 60601

Canada
  Blackwell Mosby Book Distributors
  120 Melford Drive, Scarborough, Ontario, M1B 2X4

Australia
  Blackwell Scientific Books Distributors
  (Australia) Pty Ltd, 107 Barry Street, Carlton, Victoria 3053

British Library Cataloguing in Publication Data

Illingworth, Ronald S.
Basic developmental screening.—3rd ed.
1. Infants—Growth   2. Medical screening
I. Title
612'.65   RJ131

ISBN 0–632–00945–4

First published 1973, reprinted 1975
Second edition 1977, reprinted 1979
Third edition 1982, reprinted 1984, 1985 (twice), 1986
Translated into Greek, Italian and Spanish

Set by Oxprint Ltd, Oxford and
printed and bound in Great Britain by
Express Litho Service (Oxford)

Contents

Preface to third edition

In preparing this edition I have arranged the material in a more rational order and thereby avoided some duplication. I have again taken care to avoid all unnecessary or irrelevant tests. I have increased the age cover to 4 years but I have restricted screening tests to those not requiring apparatus, apart from easily prepared material involving nothing more than firm card (with the necessary illustrations and sizes). I decided not to include the Goodenough 'draw a man' test or formboards: details of those are included in the book referred to on p. 62.

Sheffield, 1982   R. S. Illingworth

Preface to first edition

This booklet is intended to be used for screening only. It is not intended to provide an accurate score, and is not intended to be used for research purposes. It is intended to provide the busy clinic doctor, general practitioner or hospital doctor with a rapid means of eliminating anything but the mildest developmental or neurological abnormality—and of knowing when to seek the advice of an expert when in doubt.

It is written in the firm belief that many have made developmental assessment far too complicated, and that there is a need for a brief, simple, practical guide to developmental screening. For more detailed assessment and for the basis and theory of assessment I hope that the reader will refer to my book *The Development of the Infant and Young Child, Normal and Abnormal*, 7th edn, (1980) Churchill Livingstone, Edinburgh.

In this booklet I have mentioned only those features of development which are relevant and essential for screening purposes. I have aimed at keeping them to a minimum.

I have given careful consideration to material which I regard as essential and that which I regard as non-essential. *I do not consider that the elicitation of signs other than those described in this book are of value in ordinary routine developmental screening.* In particular I regard the elicitation of numerous primitive reflexes to be of no known importance for routine screening. Some may be of value to the specialist, but with rare exceptions I am sceptical even of this.

Why screen?

Every normal parent has the natural desire to know whether his child is developing normally or not. If there was some difficulty in pregnancy or labour or in the newborn period, the parent has all the more reason for wanting to know. The doctor needs to know whether the child is normal or not, if there has been a convulsion or meningitis, in order that he can allay parental anxieties, especially if the baby is late in certain aspects of development or shows unusual behaviour, facial or other physical features. He needs to assess the effect of adverse prenatal or perinatal factors, such as anoxia. To the doctor the developmental screening is part of the routine examination of any baby. He has to diagnose conditions for which treatment is available. He has to assess babies for suitability for adoption. He needs to assess the possible effects of new drugs in pregnancy or of new techniques in perinatal management.

The basis of screening

The basis of screening is the comparison of the baby's development to date with that of the normal baby—i.e. with the average, as determined by Gesell and others who studied a large number of apparently normal babies. It therefore follows that the screening must be based on a thorough knowledge of the normal.

The screening is based on the history and the physical and developmental examination and is followed by the interpretation.

Milestones of development

See Figs 1–38, pp. 10–21.

Most important milestones in italics.

Newborn   Prone—pelvis high, knees under abdomen.

2–4 weeks Watches mother intently as she speaks to him.

1 month   Ventral suspension (held prone, hand under
           abdomen)—head up momentarily, elbows
           flexed, hips partly extended, knees flexed.

4–6 weeks *Smiles at mother in response to overtures.*

6 weeks   *Ventral suspension—head help up momentarily*
           in same plane as rest of body. Some extension of
           hips and flexion of knees and elbows.
           Prone—pelvis largely flat, hips mostly extended.
           (But when sleeping the baby lies with pelvis
           high, knees under abdomen, like newborn
           baby.)
           Pull to sit from the supine—much head lag, but
           not complete; hands often open.
           Supine—follows object 90 cm away over angle
           of 90°.

2 months   Ventral suspension—maintains head in same
           plane as rest of body.
           Hands largely open.
           Prone—chin off couch. Plane of face 45° to
           couch.
           Smiles and vocalizes when talked to.
           Eyes—follow moving person.

continues on p. 22

Fig. 1. *Newborn: prone—pelvis high, knees under abdomen.*

Fig. 2. *6 weeks: prone—pelvis flat, hips extended.*

Fig. 3. *6 weeks: prone—chin intermittently lifted off couch.*

Fig. 4. *3 months: prone—weight on forearms, chest well off couch.*

Fig. 5. *6 months: prone—weight on hands, arms extended.*

Fig. 6. *10 months: creep position—hands and knees.*

Fig. 7. *1 year: walking like a bear, on soles of feet and hands.*

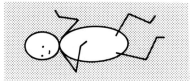

Fig. 8. *Newborn: supine, flexed position.*

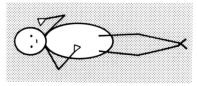

Fig. 9. *Newborn spastic: lower limbs extended.*

Fig. 10. *Newborn: ventral suspension—head held up a little, elbows flexed, hips partly extended.*

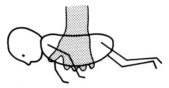

Fig. 11. *6 weeks: ventral suspension—head held up momentarily in same plane as rest of body. Hips extended.*

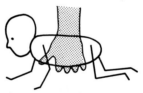

Fig. 12. *10 weeks: ventral suspension—head held up well beyond plane of rest of body.*

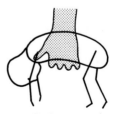

Fig. 13. *2 months: abnormal baby in ventral suspension—arms and legs hang down.*

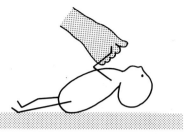

Fig. 14. *Newborn: pulled to sit—almost complete head lag.*

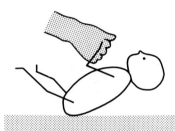

Fig. 15. *2 months: pulled to sit—less head lag.*

(N.B.)

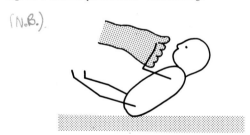

Fig. 16. *4 months: pulled to sit—no head lag.*

Fig. 17. *5 months: when about to be pulled up, lifts head.*

Fig. 18. *6 months: supine—spontaneously elevates head.*

Fig. 19. *Newborn: held sitting—fully rounded back.*

Fig. 20. *1 month: held sitting—lifts head up intermittently.*

Fig. 21. *2 months: held sitting—back straightening; head up.*

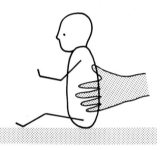

Fig. 22. *4 months: held sitting—head well up, steady, back nearly straight.*

Fig. 23. *6 months: sits with hands forward for support.*

Fig. 24. *8 months: sitting steadily, no support.*

Fig. 25. *11 months: sits and pivots.*

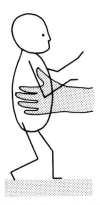

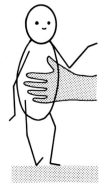

Fig. 26. *3 months: held standing—sags at knees and hips.*

Fig. 27. *6 months: held standing—bears full weight.*

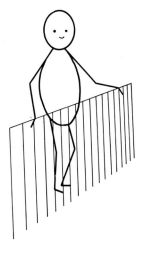

Fig. 28. *9 months: stands—holding on to playpen.*

Fig. 29. *11 months: walks—2 hands held.*

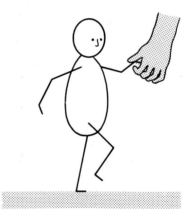

Fig. 30. *1 year: walks—1 hand held.*

Fig. 31. *13 months: walks—no support.*

Fig. 32. *6 months: transfers from 1 hand to another.*

Fig. 33. *6 months: palmar grasp of cube.*

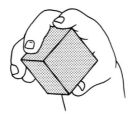

Fig. 34. *8 months: grasp, intermediate.*

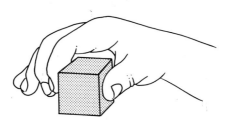

Fig. 35. *1 year: mature grasp of cube.*

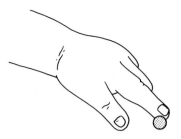

Fig. 36. *9–10 months: index finger approach to object.*

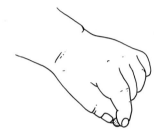

Fig. 37. *9–10 months: finger thumb apposition—pellet picked up between tip of forefinger and tip of thumb.*

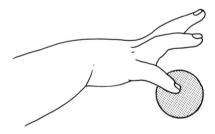

Fig. 38. *6 months (or older): spastic approach to object—splaying out of hand.*

3 months	Ventral suspension—holds head up long time beyond plane of rest of body.
	Prone—plane of face 45°–90° from couch.
	Pulled to sit—only slight head lag.
	Hands loosely open.
	Holds rattle placed in hand.
	Vocalizes a great deal when talked to.
	Follows object for 180° (lying supine).
	Turns head to sound (3–4 months) on a level with the ear.
4 months	Prone—plane of face at 90° to couch.
	Hands come together.
	Pulls dress over face.
	Laughs aloud.
5 months	Prone—weight on forearms.
	Pulled to sit—no head lag.
	Supine—feet to mouth. Plays with toes.
	Able to go for object and get it.
6 months	Prone—weight on hands, extended arms.
	Pulled to sit—no head lag.
	Supine—lifts head spontaneously.
	Sits on floor, hands forward for support.
	Held in standing position—full weight on legs.
	Rolls, prone to supine, completely over.
	Begins to imitate (e.g. a cough).
	Chews.
	Transfers cube from 1 hand to another.
7 months	*Sits on floor seconds, no support.*
	Rolls, supine to prone, completely over.
	Held standing—bounces.
	Feeds self with biscuit.
	Attracts attention by cough or other method.
	Turns head to sound below level of ear.

8 months	Sits unsupported. Leans forward to reach objects. Turns head to sound above level of ear.
9 months	Stands, holding on. Pulls to stand or sitting position. *Crawls on abdomen.*
9–10 months	*Index finger approach.* *Finger thumb apposition*—picks pellet between tip of thumb and tip of forefinger.
10 months	*Creeps, hands and knees, abdomen off couch.* Can change from sitting to prone and back. Pulls self to sitting position. *Waves bye.* *Plays pat-a-cake.* *Helps to dress*—holding arm out for coat, foot for shoe, or transferring object from 1 hand to another for sleeve.
11 months	*Offers object to mother, but will not release it.* One word with meaning. Sitting—pivots round without overbalancing. Walks, holding on to furniture; walks, 2 hands held.
One year	2–3 words with meaning. Prone—walks on hands and feet like bear. Walks, 1 hand held. Casting objects, 1 after another, begins. *Gives brick to mother.*
13 months	*Walks, no support.* *Mouthing of objects largely stopped.* Slobbering largely stopped.
15 months	Creeps up stairs. Kneels. Takes off shoes.

Feeds self, picking up an ordinary cup, drinking, putting it down.
Imitation of mother in domestic work ('domestic mimicry').
Jargon.
Cubes—tower of 2.

18 months   *No more casting.*
Gets up and down stairs, holding rail.
Jumps, both feet.
Seats self in chair.
Toilet control—tells mother that he wants potty. Largely dry by day.
Throws ball without falling.
Takes off gloves, socks, unzips.
Manages spoon well.
Points to 3 parts of body on request.
Book—turns pages, 2 or 3 at a time.
Points to some objects, on request.
Cubes—tower of 3–4.
Pencil and paper—imitates stroke (examiner gets child to watch stroke being made and asks child to do the same). Picture card—identifies 1. (Where is the?)

21–24 months   *Spontaneously joins 2 or 3 words together to make sentence.*

2 years   Picks up object from floor without falling.
Runs.
Kicks ball without overbalancing.
Turns door knob, unscrews end.
Cubes—tower of 6 or 7.
Puts on shoes, socks, pants; takes off shoes, socks.
Points to 4 parts of body on request.
Pencil—imitates vertical and circular strokes.
Book—turns pages singly.
Mainly dry at night.

Climbs stairs, 2 feet per step.
Cubes—imitates train but forgets chimney.
Picture card—identifies 5 (Where is the?),
names 3 (What is this?).

2½ years   Knows full name, sex.
Cubes—tower of 8. Imitates train with chimney.
Picture card—identifies 7, names 5.
Pencil and paper—imitates vertical and
horizontal stroke.
Digits (say after me, eg. 825). 3 trials
(different figures in each trial).
2 in 1 of 3 trials
Coloured forms—places 1 correctly.

3 years   Dresses and undresses fully, except shoe laces.
Cubes—tower of 9. Imitates bridge.
Pencil and paper—imitates cross (i.e. watching
examiner make 1).
Pencil and paper—copies circle (i.e. copies
previously prepared circle).
Picture card—names 8.
Digits—3 in 1 of 3 trials.
Coloured forms—3 correct.
Uncoloured forms—4 correct.

3½ years   Cubes—tower of 10. Copies bridge (i.e.
examiner made bridge out of sight of child).
Picture card—names 10.
Digits—3 correct in 2 of 3 trials.
Uncoloured forms—6.

4 years   Cubes—imitates gate.
Pencil and paper—copies train.
Digits—3 in 3 of 3 trials.
Coloured forms—all correct.
Uncoloured forms—8.

Age for screening

The easiest ages at which to screen babies are 6 weeks, 6 months and 10 months. This is because there are readily assessable features of development at those ages. The most difficult age at which to screen after the newborn period is 3 to 4 months, and I prefer not to assess a baby at 8 months. In a baby clinic the age of screening is dictated in part by the immunization procedures. From the age of 1 to about 3 it is particularly difficult, because children are coy, shy and in the phase of negativism.

General history

The history must include:
  Birth weight and duration of gestation.
  Prenatal risk factors—infections, illness, bleeding, hypertension, etc.
  Genetic factors—mental subnormality, degenerative disease of the nervous system, psychoses.
  Familial pattern of development if the child is late in certain fields.
  Perinatal factors—fetal distress, abnormal presentation, labour, delivery, condition at birth—anoxia, convulsions.
  Postnatal—development (e.g. age of beginning to smile, etc.).
  Sucking or swallowing difficulties, undue drowsiness, irritability, crying.
  Illness. Emotional deprivation.
  The previous development of the baby has to be determined. In order to assess the previous rate of development one needs to know whether there are signs that a child who

has had a bad start is showing accelerated development (and may therefore catch up to the normal), slowing of development (as in degenerative diseases of the nervous system) or signs of deterioration in performance. One must know whether there has been any illness or other factor such as emotional deprivation which may have retarded his development. The 'risk' factors will be named in the relevant sections to follow.

If there is delay in development, a history of the familial pattern of development is important. For instance, if the child is late in sitting and walking, and is normal in other aspects of development, one may find that the father or mother was similarly late in walking.

Developmental history

It is essential that the doctor and mother should each understand what the other means and says. One assesses the mother's understanding, memory and veracity as she replies, and when in doubt comes back and asks the same question in a different way. The questions to be asked depend on the age of the child: it would not be profitable to ask the mother of a 5 year old, 1 of her 10 children, when he began to smile. It is not enough to ask *whether* he shows a particular skill. One needs to know *when* he began to show it.

The developmental history is a good comparative check on one's own objective findings. The following are suggested questions when the child is of a relevant age:
1   Does he smile at you when you talk to him? I mean only when you talk to him. When did he begin? (Av. 4–6 weeks.) Some mothers have the extraordinary idea that pain from wind makes babies smile. They may interpret any facial movement in sleep as a smile: or else they stroke the lips or face and interpret a facial movement as a smile. The doctor is interested only in the smile in response to social overture.
2   Does he make little cooing noises as well as smile when

you talk to him? When did he begin? (Av. a week or 2 after smiling begins.) Later, when doubtful about possible backwardness, one asks, 'Does he smile much?' A backward child at 6 months may smile only occasionally.

3   Will he hold a rattle if you put it in the hand? How long? When did he begin? (Av. 3–4 months.)

4   Does he turn his head when he hears noises? When did he begin? (Av. 3–4 months.)

5   Will he reach out for a toy and get it without it being put into the hand? When did he begin? (Av. 5 months.) If one has difficulty in eliciting the response with the cube, ask 'Would he be able to get hold of tnis without it being put into the hand?'

6   Have you seen him take a toy from one hand into the other? When did he begin? (Av. 6 months.)

7   Can he chew yet? I do not mean 'suck'. Does he make chewing movements with the jaw? Can he manage to eat a biscuit? When did he begin? (Av. 6–7 months.) (This is nothing to do with teething.)

8   Can he sit on the floor without support? When did he begin to sit for a few seconds on the floor without help? (Av., with hands forward for support—6 months; with no support, for seconds—7 months.) (*Note.* This is very different from sitting in the pram, with support round the buttocks, etc.)

9   Does he copy you in anything that you do? If the mother says 'yes', ask her what he does. He may imitate a noise, razzing or a cough, or putting the tongue out. When did he begin? (Av. 6–7 months.)

10   Will he stand, holding on to the furniture? When did he begin? (Av. 8 months.)

11   Will he pull himself up to the standing position at the side of the furniture? When did he begin? (Av. 9 months.)

12   Does he crawl (on his tummy) (av. 9 months) or creep (hands and knees) (av. 10 months)? When did he begin?

13   Does he walk, holding on to the furniture ('cruise')? When did he begin? (Av. 10 months.)

14   Will he wave bye-bye? When did he begin? (Av. 9 months.)

15 Will he play pat-a-cake (clap hands)? When did he begin? (Av. 9 months.)

16 Does he say any words with meaning? (Av. 10–11 months.) If the mother claims that he says 'dada' one asks, 'Does he really mean daddy? Is it when daddy is not there or only when he is there?'

17 Does he help you to dress him? If the answer is 'yes', ask what he does. One means that he holds his arm out for a coat, foot out for a shoe, or passes an object from 1 hand into the other in order to put his arm into a sleeve. When did he begin? (Av. 10 months.)

18 Can he manage an ordinary cup—to pick it up, drink from it and put it down—without you helping him? When did he begin? (Av. 15 months.) Does he feed himself fully without help? (Av. 15–18 months.)

19 Can he dress himself or undress himself at all? What can he get on or off? When did he begin? (Av., shoes and socks off at 15 months; takes off gloves, socks, unzips at 18 months; puts on shoes, socks, pants at 2 years.)

20 Does he tell you when he wants to use the potty? When did he begin? (Av. 18 months.) Is he usually dry by day? (Av. 18–24 months.) By night? (Av. 2–3 years.)

21 Does he copy you doing things about the house—brushing, sweeping, washing up? (Domestic mimicry.) When did he begin? (Av. 15 months.)

22 Does he join 2 or 3 words together (not just imitating you)? When did he begin? (Av. 21–24 months.)

If in doubt about a child's hearing, ask 'Will he come from another room if called—without his seeing you call him?'

If in doubt about his being backward in speech—ask 'Does he understand what you say to him? Could he point out objects in pictures if you ask him?' (Understanding of words always precedes the ability to articulate them.)

If in doubt about his being backward, and if he has older siblings at school, ask, 'How does he compare with his brother, apart from his speech?' (if he is late in talking). What about his general understanding, his intelligence? Then ask, 'Is his brother doing well at school?' (in case he is also backward).

Physical and developmental examination

The physical and developmental examination must include examination for congenital abnormalities, such as limb deformities, cleft palate or congenital heart disease, because a child with any major congenital abnormality is more liable than others to be mentally below average. It will include examination for subluxation or dislocation of the hip (p. 57). It must include the maximum head circumference in relation to the baby's weight.

GENERAL

Equipment
The equipment needed for the physical examination is a stethoscope, patellar hammer (a small one, preferably with a triangular piece of rubber at the tapping end), a non-stretch tape-measure (for many tape-measures stretch and become inaccurate), a head circumference chart, and a

Fig. 39. *Two 'picture cards' (30 × 22½ cm).*

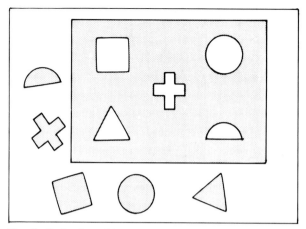

Fig. 40. *Red 'coloured forms', cut out of cardboard. (Whole card measures 30 × 22½ cm; shapes to correspond, e.g. the square measures 5 × 5 cm.)*

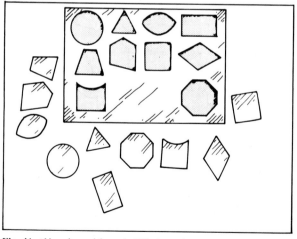

Fig. 41. *'Uncoloured forms'. (Whole card measures 30 × 22½ cm; shapes to correspond, e.g. the square measures 5 × 5 cm.)*

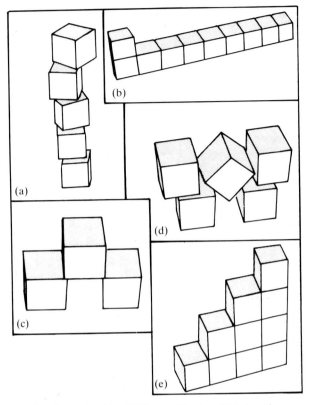

Fig. 42. *One inch cubes. (a) Tower of 5 cubes; (b) train with chimney; (c) bridge; (d) gate; (e) steps.*

weight and height chart (with centiles). Scales for weighing should be checked for accuracy at intervals.

The essential equipment for developmental screening is 10 one inch cubes (only 2 or 3 are needed in the 1st year), a fairly blunt-ended pencil and paper, a picture card (Fig. 39), and coloured and uncoloured cut-out shapes to fit into corresponding places on the card (Figs 40–41). Figure 42 shows the tower, train, bridge, gate and steps constructed from the cubes.

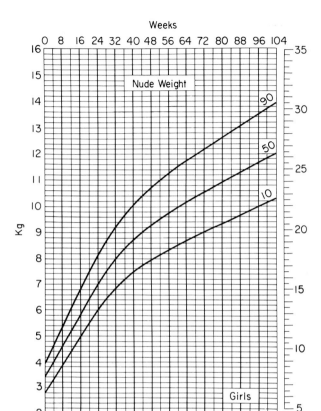

Fig. 43. *Weight of girls.*

Head circumference (Figs 43–45, Tables 1–2)
The maximum head circumference must be determined in
all babies as a routine because the head size depends on the
growth of the cranial contents. If the brain does not grow
normally the head circumference is likely to be small and so
suggests a brain defect. On the other hand an unusually

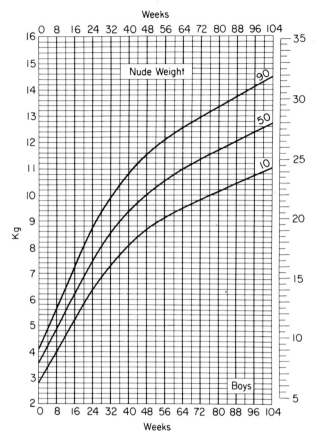

Fig. 44. *Weight of boys.*

large head may indicate hydrocephalus or other disease. In all cases the head circumference must be related to the baby's weight, for a big baby is likely to have a bigger head than a small baby, and a small baby a smaller head than a big baby. When in doubt the head circumference and the weight should be plotted on the centile charts: they should more or less correspond in their placing—though there is the unlikely

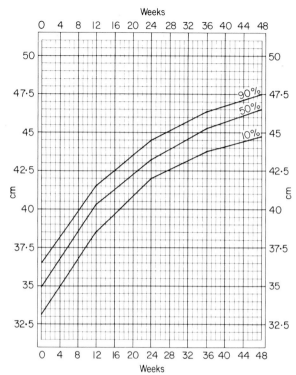

Fig. 45. *Head circumference.*

possibility that there is a familial tendency to an unusually large or small head.

The following are the causes of a child having an unusually large head:

Normal variation, often familial.

Big baby.

Hydrocephalus.

Hydranencephaly.

Megalencephaly.

Subdural effusion.

Cerebral tumour.

The following are the causes of a child having an unusually small head:

Normal variation, often familial.

Small baby.

Mental deficiency.

Craniostenosis.

Table 1a. *Head circumference in relation to birth weight.* (After Usher R. & McLean F. (1969) *J. Pediatr.* **74,** 901.)

Birth weight (g)	Head circumference (cm)
1000	24.5
1200	26.2
1400	27.7
1600	29.0
1800	30.1
2000	31.0
2200	31.8
2400	32.5
2600	33.1
2800	33.6
3000	34.1
3200	34.5
3400	34.9
3600	35.2
3800	35.5
4000	35.8

Table 1b. *Mean birth weight at different gestation periods.*

Duration of gestation (weeks)	Mean birth weight (g)
26	933
28	1113
30	1373
32	1727
34	2113
36	2589
38	3133
40	3480

Table 2. *Weight (g) and head circumference (cm).*

| | 10th centile | | 50th centile | | 90th centile | |
	Head	Weight	Head	Weight	Head	Weight
Age of boys						
Birth	33.5	2.8	35.0	3.5	36.0	4.1
3 months	39.3	5.0	40.6	5.9	42.1	7.0
6 months	42.0	6.8	43.8	7.9	45.0	9.2
9 months	43.6	7.9	45.7	9.2	47.2	10.6
1 year	44.5	8.8	46.8	10.2	48.5	11.7
2 years	47.1	11.0	49.1	12.7	50.9	14.6
Age of girls						
Birth	33.6	2.9	35.0	3.4	35.6	4.0
3 months	38.1	4.8	39.7	5.6	40.9	6.4
6 months	41.2	6.4	42.9	6.9	44.2	8.5
9 months	43.2	7.6	44.6	8.7	46.2	10.0
1 year	44.4	8.4	45.7	9.7	47.2	11.2
2 years	46.2	10.4	48.0	12.2	49.3	14.1

Muscle tone

This is assessed mainly by the following tests:

1 Assessing the range of movement, especially in abduction of the hip and in dorsiflexion of the ankle. The range of movement is increased in hypotonia and decreased in hypertonia.

2 Feeling the resistance to passive movement, especially in the elbows, hips, knees and ankles. Voluntary resistance by the patient may confuse the assessment.

3 Shaking the limb. One holds the leg below the knee and rapidly shakes the limb in order to observe the amount of movement at the ankle. If the limb is hypertonic, there will be little or no movement in the foot. If the limb is hypotonic, there will be excessive movement. The same test is applied to the upper limb, holding it below the elbow and observing the movement in the hand.

The tendon jerks and plantar responses

For testing the tendon jerks I prefer a small patellar hammer with a triangular rubber end-piece for tapping the tendon. One begins testing for the knee jerk by tapping over the dorsum of the ankle, and tapping at intervals up the leg until the patellar tendon is reached. The heel must be resting on the couch and the limb relaxed at the moment of tapping. A brisk response when tapping over the lower part of the leg means only that the jerk is brisk, but not necessarily abnormal. If it is brisk, there will commonly be a few flickers of ankle clonus. Ankle clonus is tested by a rapid but gentle dorsiflexion of the ankle with the hip partly abducted and the knee flexed. If one suspects that the upper limbs may be spastic, one tests for exaggeration of the biceps jerk by beginning over the shoulder and tapping down the upper arm at intervals until the biceps tendon is reached. One taps the tendon itself, without one's thumb in between. A brisk response over the upper arm means only that other signs of cerebral palsy should be looked for.

The plantar response is elicited by *gentle* stimulation of the distal half of the outside of the foot with the *thumb*, *never* with a key or pin. One must never convey the stimulus across the sole of the foot, for that elicits the plantar grasp reflex (flexor). *The plantar response in normal infants is flexor.*

DIFFERENT AGES

The newborn .

I propose to discuss the assessment of the newborn only briefly, because the assessment lies more in the hands of the paediatrician resident in the obstetrics unit than in the hands of doctors for whom this book is designed.

In an obstetrics unit the assessment of the maturity of the newborn infant may be of the greatest importance if there is doubt about the duration of gestation. The method of assessment has been fully described by me in my book *The Development of The Infant and Young Child, Normal and Abnormal*, 7th edn (1980) Churchill Livingstone, Edinburgh: it was based on the work of Dubowitz, and does not lend itself to abbreviation.

The condition of the child at birth can be conveniently assessed by the method of Virginia Apgar, based on the heart rate, respirations, muscle tone, reflex irritability and colour, 1 minute and 4 minutes after birth. The scoring method is shown in Table 3.

Table 3. *Scoring method for assessing the condition of a child at birth.*

Score	Heart rate	Respiratory effort	Muscle tone	Colour	Reflex
2	Over 100	Strong cry	Good, active movement	Completely pink	Irritability (Response to stimulation of foot) Normal cry
1	Below 100	Slow, irregular respirations	Fair, some flexion of limbs	Baby pink, limbs blue	Moderately depressed grimace
0	No beat obtained	No respirations	Flaccid	Blue, pale	Absent

A score of 10 denotes an excellent clinical condition. A low score denotes a poor condition. The method should only be used in conjunction with other methods of assessment.

The baby is inspected as he lies in his crib.

Note:
1 The posture—especially undue extension of the limbs, as in cerebral palsy.
2 The quality, quantity and symmetry of movements—for the child with severe cerebral palsy is relatively immobile, while the child with spastic hemiplegia may exhibit asymmetry of movement.
3 The nature of the cry: the high pitched cry of the child with cerebral irritability is readily recognized.
4 The baby's alertness.
5 The face (the facies of disease or facial palsy).
6 The eyes—for nystagmus or opacity.
Palpate the anterior fontanelle and sutures—the fontanelle for evidence of undue tension, and sutures for separation.

Estimate the muscle tone.

Test the Moro reflex. It is elicited by pulling the child up from the supine to an angle of 45° from the couch, with one's hand behind the head, and suddenly releasing one's hold of the head. The absence of the Moro reflex is usually of serious significance, and occurs in kernicterus. Asymmetry of the Moro reflex occurs in brachial plexus injury (Erb's palsy) and fracture of the clavicle or humerus.

The Moro reflex consists of abduction and extension of the arms, opening of the hands, followed by adduction of the arms as if an embrace.

Examine the mouth (for cleft palate), the heart, chest, abdomen, umbilicus, hips, the back for a congenital dermal sinus and the testes for their descent.

Screening at 6 weeks

The baby is on his mother's knees with nothing on but a nappy: this is removed as soon as he is lifted from her knee.

HISTORY REQUIRED

Prenatal and natal factors (p. 26).

Condition of baby to date.

History of smiling (or, if no smile, watching the mother) and vocalizing.

Sucking and swallowing difficulties.

Excess crying, sleepiness, irritability.

EXAMINATION

Note facial appearance, skull size and shape, alertness. Observe him as mother talks to him.

Feel the anterior fontanelle for undue bulging, and if in doubt about the fontanelle, feel the sutures to eliminate undue separation.

Listen to the heart.

Lift the baby from the mother's knee after removing the nappy.

Inspect the back for a congenital dermal sinus. If it is in the lumbar region or above, it may communicate with the sub-arachnoid space and cause meningitis.

Hold in ventral suspension—to assess motor development.

Place in the prone position—to assess motor development.

Place in the supine position and pull to the sitting position—to assess motor development.

Test weight bearing.

Inspect the baby's eyes—for fixed squint, opacity, nystagmus.

Examine the mouth for monilia infection.

Inspect the umbilicus. Palpate the abdomen.

Examine the testes for descent.

Examine the hip for the range of abduction.

Estimate muscle tone—by shaking the limbs, feeling the resistance to passive movement, dorsiflexing the ankles—at the same time testing for ankle clonus.

Test the knee jerks and plantar responses.

Return to the mother's knee.

Measure the maximum head circumference. (It is assumed that his naked weight has been recorded.) When in doubt, plot the head circumference and weight on the centile charts for comparison.

Test the hearing. (This may be routine only after the 3rd month: but when assessment is of particular importance, as for adoption, it must be routine even in the young baby.)

Normally the whole examination will take between 1 and 2 minutes. It will take much longer if any doubt arises about 1 or more of the findings.

Screening at 6 months
The baby is on his mother's knee with nothing on but his nappy.

HISTORY REQUIRED

Prenatal and natal factors if not already in notes.

Condition of baby to date: illnesses; hospital stay; any relevant environmental factors, such as emotional deprivation.

Age of onset of:

Smiling.

Vocalization.
Holding rattle placed in hand.
Turning head to sound.
Reaching out and getting object.
Imitation.
Chewing.
Sitting.

Observe:
Facial expression.
Alertness, responsiveness and interest in surroundings.
His smile when one talks to him.
Vocalizations.
Skull size and shape.
Eyes—for squint, nystagmus, opacity.
Palpate the anterior fontanelle for bulging. (The age at which it closes is unimportant.)
Test the hearing.
Offer 2 one inch cubes and observe the nature of his grasp: observe transfer. Possibly test for distant vision (p. 59).
Take him from his mother's knee, after removing his nappy, and place him on his back (supine) on the couch.
Pull him to the sitting position. Note feeling of resistance or repeated tendency to fall back (when placed sitting forward), or spasm of hamstrings with flexion of the knees, as he is pulled to the sitting position (as in spasticity).
Note ability to sit with hands forward for support, or unsupported.
Examine hips for abduction.
Test muscle tone, knee jerks, plantar responses, dorsiflexion of the ankles—and observe ankle clonus.
Test weight bearing on the legs.
Note prone position.
Examine heart, palpate abdomen, inspect mouth, examine testes.
Measure head circumference: if in doubt mark it and the weight on the centile charts for comparison.

Screening at 10 months

The baby is on his mother's knee, wearing only his nappy.

History as before, if not already taken.
In addition—age of onset of:

    Standing holding on.
    Pulling self to stand.
    Pulling self to sit.
    Walking, holding on.
    Crawling, creeping.
    Waving bye-bye, playing pat-a-cake.
    Helping to dress.
    Words with meaning.

EXAMINATION

Observe:

    Facial expression.
    Alertness, responsiveness and interest in surroundings.
    Skull size and shape.
    Vocalizations.
    Eyes—for squint, nystagmus, opacity.

Test the hearing.

Offer a pellet of paper—to observe the index finger approach, finger–thumb apposition. One must be certain that one has elicited the maximum performance here: when in doubt one offers the pellet repeatedly in order to be sure that one is not underestimating the baby's manipulative development. (The younger baby 'rakes' for the pellet and gets it in the palm of his hand, and later at the base of the thumb and forefinger or between other fingers.)

Offer 2 bricks. Again note the index finger approach. At 10 months he may 'match' the cubes—bringing the 2 together as if comparing them. Possibly test distant vision.

Take him from his mother, after removing the nappy.

Place him on his back: palpate the abdomen; test the hip abduction, knee jerks, muscle tone, dorsiflexion of ankles, plantar responses. Note any feeling of resistance to pulling him up to the sitting position, as in spasticity, with a repeated tendency to fall back when placed sitting forward, and spasm of the hamstrings.

Test his steadiness in the sitting position.

Place him in the prone position to observe whether he lies on his abdomen or gets into the creep position.

Test weight bearing on the legs.

Examine the heart, palpate the abdomen and testes, inspect the mouth.

Measure the head circumference: if in doubt mark it and the weight on the centile charts for comparison.

Screening at 18 months

HISTORY REQUIRED

As before, if not already taken. In addition ask:

How many words he says with meaning.

Whether he is joining any words together, other than in imitation. When he began.

When he walked without help.

When he was able to feed himself fully, managing an ordinary cup, picking it up, drinking and putting it down without help.

How much he can dress and undress himself.

Whether he tells the mother that he wants the potty, when he began, and when he was usually dry—by day or by night.

When he began domestic mimicry.

If he seems backward, ask how long he will play with 1 toy. (Distinguish the obsessional play of a defective child with 1 toy.)

EXAMINATION

Observe facial expression, alertness, responsiveness, interest in surroundings, skull size and shape, jargon, speech.

Observe mouthing, slobbering, casting—all probably abnormal at this age.

Observe the eyes—squint, nystagmus, opacity.

44

Test the hearing.

Only test for the index finger approach and finger–thumb apposition if he is backward.

Offer 6 bricks: show him how to build a tower.

Ask him to point to parts of the body, or his shoe, or to fetch a ball.

Test for distant vision.

Take him from his mother, after removing the nappy.

Test hip abduction, muscle tone, knee jerks, plantar responses.

Examine the heart, palpate the abdomen and testes.

Observe his gait as he walks.

Measure the head circumference, as before.

Screening at 2 years

HISTORY REQUIRED

As before, if not already taken; exclude developmental history prior to 6 months.

In addition the age of onset of:

    Joining words together.

    Toilet training: dryness day and night.

    Ability to dress self: how much he can do.

    Ability to feed self.

EXAMINATION

As 18 month child.

If speech is delayed, ask whether he understands everything said to him, whether he can hear and whether he will come from another room if called without seeing the mother call him.

Offer 6 cubes. Make a train of 5 with a chimney and ask him to do the same: he is unlikely to add the chimney.

Observe mouthing, slobbering or casting (all abnormal at this age.)

Ask him to point to parts of the body.

Interpretation

The following factors *must* be taken into consideration:

1 Allowance for prematurity

If, for instance, a child has been born 2 months early, he has missed 2 months' development in utero. Hence if one is assessing him 6 months after birth, one has to compare him not with an average 6-month-old baby, but with a 4-month-old baby.

2 Familial factors

If there is anything unusual about a child's development, one should note a relevant unusual familial pattern of development. For instance, if a child is late in motor development, but normal in all other aspects of development, a familial pattern of lateness in learning to walk is likely to be relevant.

3 Relative importance of different fields of development

Some fields of development are more important than others for the overall assessment. Gross motor development (sitting and walking), are the least important: some mentally subnormal children learn to sit and walk at the usual age. Manipulative development, the use of the hands, is much more important. Of the greatest importance is the child's alertness, interest in surroundings, responsiveness and concentration. Teething is of no importance in assessment.

4 Range of normality

It is impossible to state the normal range of development, because it is always impossible to draw the line between normal and abnormal: but the further away from the average a child is in any measurement, the less likely he is to be normal. The figures below refer to full-term babies and children seen by me.

Smiling	3 days to about 7 weeks.
Sitting, no support for seconds	5 months to one year.
Walking, no help	8 months to 4 years.
Bladder control at night	15 months to 10 years +.
Speech, sentences	10 months to 5 years +.

Note. Some children never creep or crawl. About 10 per cent shuffle on hand and buttock at the beginning of the usual walking age.

5 Lateness in certain fields of development

Below is a summary of causes of lateness in certain fields of development.

Late sitting	Familial feature.
	Mental subnormality.
	Hypotonia or hypertonia (cerebral palsy).
	Environmental factors—baby kept lying down. Emotional deprivation.
	Delayed motor maturation.
Late walking	Familial feature.
	Mental subnormality.
	Hypotonia or hypertonia.
	Delayed motor maturation.
	Environmental factors—baby kept lying down. Emotional deprivation.
	Personality—fear of falls.
	Muscular dystrophy.
	Not due to dislocated hip, obesity.
Late speech	Familial feature.
	Unexplained delay.
	Mental subnormality.
	Deafness.
	Autism.
	Environmental factors—no one talking to child.
	Twins.
	Not due to laziness, tongue tie, 'everything being done for him'.
Late sphincter control	Familial feature.
	Unexplained delay.
	Delayed maturation.
	Mental subnormality.

Mismanagement of toilet training and other
environmental factors.

Organic causes—e.g. ureterocele, meningomyelocele, urethral valves (male),
ectopic ureter (female).

6 Minimum developmental level

It is useful to fix in one's mind the minimum developmental
level in different aspects of development. For instance, a
baby who spontaneously lifts his head from the supine cannot be less than the 6 months level of motor development: a
baby who transfers an object from 1 hand to another
cannot be less than the 6 months level in manipulation:
a baby who shows the index finger approach and finger–
thumb apposition cannot be less than the 9–10 months level
of manipulative development—and because of the relative
importance of this, his overall intellectual level can hardly
be less than the 9–10 month level.

7 Objective findings versus mother's opinion

One compares one's own objective findings with the
mother's history of the baby's development. In my experience they nearly always tally well. If there is a discrepancy,
one should look for the reason—and if necessary retest.

8 Previous rate of development

One assesses the mother's story of his previous milestones in
order to assess his previous rate of development. If he had
been a slow starter, his milestones may show an acceleration
in development. If he is now backward the previous milestones may show a slowing down in development, pointing
possibly to a degenerative disease.

9 Factors retarding examination performance

One considers whether the child's performance was less
than he was possibly capable of achieving—perhaps because
he was tired, hungry, distracted, poorly or for other reasons
not co-operating well.

10 Other factors affecting development

One notes all factors which may have affected his development, or which are still affecting it, and which have no
relevance to his overall potential. For instance, when a baby
of 6 months bears no weight on the legs, the commonest

cause is the mother's failure to allow the baby to bear the weight on his legs.

If the child has a physical handicap, such as meningo-myelocele, blindness or deafness, the relevant skills will be greatly affected, but they have little or no relevance to his overall intellectual potential. In the assessment, one excludes tests which are affected by his particular handicap.

11 Significance of risk factors

If after assessment the child is normal, the 'risk factors' are usually ignored but if there are doubtful aspects of development, an additional risk factor increases the likelihood that all is not well: for instance, a baby who was born prematurely, of a very low birth weight, is 'at risk' of having cerebral palsy. If on assessment at the equivalent of 6 weeks (having allowed for prematurity) one finds increased muscle tone and delayed motor development, there are then 3 factors which suggest that the child may have cerebral palsy. The 'risk factor' alerts one to be particularly careful in the examination of the relevant aspects of development, and serves as an additional factor if clinical examination raises doubts about the baby's normality.

12 Significance of head circumference

The head circumference in relation to the weight is an essential part of the examination. If it is normal, then doubtful aspects of one's findings assume less importance: one would be particularly loath to diagnose mental subnormality if the relative head circumference were normal in relation to weight. On the other hand if the head circumference is notably small in relation to the weight, and it is not a familial feature, slight backwardness in 1 or 2 fields of development would strongly suggest the likelihood that the child is not up to the average in potential.

13 Limitation of developmental assessment

It is futile to attempt to give a single figure and call it the IQ. One can legitimately refer to a baby's overall performance as the DQ—the developmental quotient, which indicates his present performance in relation to his age and the average performance of babies of that age. One must then remember that his performance will be profoundly modified by his home, teaching, neighbourhood, personality, opportunity, health, nutrition and many other factors. A sensible way to report one's findings is as follows: 'The overall performance of this 24-month-old child is that of an average 30-month-old child, with some scatter in the range of 27 to 36 months. He is therefore above average in development'.

All these factors *must* be considered. *He who thinks that a sensible developmental screening can be made on purely objective findings on the basis of some psychologist's tests reveals a regrettable lack of understanding of the complexities of human development.*

In making the final assessment one puts all the findings in the history, physical and developmental examination, and all the above 13 factors into one's cerebral computer—and reaches a conclusion.

Mental subnormality

'Risk factors', which increase the likelihood that a child may be mentally retarded, are mainly:

Prenatal
: Low birth weight, especially in relation to the duration of gestation.
  Prematurity, especially when extreme.
  Family history of mental subnormality.
  Virus infections in early pregnancy.
  Pelvic irradiation.

Natal
: Severe perinatal anoxia.
  Neonatal convulsions, especially if due to hypoglycaemia.
  Hyperbilirubinaemia.

Postnatal
: Hypoglycaemic fits.
  Pyogenic meningitis.
  Lead poisoning.
  Emotional deprivation.
  Severe head injury.

The mentally subnormal infant is late in all aspects of development, except occasionally in gross motor development (sitting and walking): he is relatively more advanced in sitting and walking than in other fields unless there is associated cerebral palsy, in which case he will be more retarded in motor development than in other fields. He is relatively more retarded in responsiveness, alertness and interest in surroundings, and later in speech, than in other fields. Mental subnormality can never be diagnosed on the basis of retardation in single fields of development.

There is usually a small head circumference in relation to the weight: but there may be hydrocephalus.

There are often other congenital anomalies (such as congenital heart disease, cleft palate, syndactyly).

As he is late in all fields of development, with the occasional exceptions noted, the following are some of the developmental features of the mentally subnormal infant:

1   In the newborn period, he is more likely to have sucking, swallowing and feeding difficulties.

2   He sleeps more than most normal babies. Mothers often describe their defective babies as being 'so good, not a bit of trouble'.

3   He is late in:

Smiling in response to his mother, and subsequently in vocalizing.

Following with his eyes and in turning his head to sound. His response is slow.

Reaching out for objects and getting them.

Learning to chew.

Imitating, e.g. a cough, pat-a-cake, waving bye-bye.

Helping his mother to dress him.

Ceasing to take toys and other objects to the mouth.

Later (after the 1st birthday) ceasing to 'cast' (throw) one object after another onto the floor (normally stopped after about 15 months).

4   *He shows poor interest in his surroundings, less alertness and responsiveness than normal babies. He is too easily distracted so that he does not concentrate, e.g. on trying to reach an object.*

Diagnostic snares

1 The child may be tired, hungry or ill at the time of the assessment so that his performance is deceptively poor.

2 There are great normal variations in development. Some are 'slow starters'—apparently backward in the early days, yet proving to be normal later.

3 A child may be retarded because of emotional deprivation. The effect of this may be reversible if he is placed in a good home (e.g. a foster home).

4 He may have an unrecognized sensory defect—visual or auditory—causing apparent backwardness.

Mental deterioration

The following are the main causes of either slowing in development or mental deterioration:

Malnutrition in infancy.

Emotional deprivation. Child abuse.

Hyperbilirubinaemia, neonatal.

Metabolic diseases—phenylketonuria, other abnormal amino-acidurias, lipoidoses, mucopolysaccharidoses.

Hypothyroidism.

Hypoglycaemia.

Hypernatraemia.

Lead poisoning.

Epilepsy, and overdose of antiepileptic drugs.

Degenerative diseases of the nervous system.

Meningitis.

Cerebral vascular accidents.

Severe head injury.

Psychoses.

Anoxia.

Mongols are developmentally more advanced in the early weeks. Their development slows down in the 2nd half of the 1st year.

Cerebral palsy
(See Figs 9, 13, 38)

There are all degrees of severity of cerebral palsy. The mildest forms cannot be diagnosed in infancy, but there should be no difficulty in diagnosing the moderate or severe forms in early infancy, especially those of the spastic variety.

History
Certain factors increase the risk that a child will have cerebral palsy. They are mainly:

1 Prematurity, especially extreme, or extreme low birth weight in relation to the duration of gestation.
2 Multiple pregnancy.
3 Mental subnormality.
4 Severe perinatal anoxia.
5 Severe hyperbilirubinaemia in the newborn period (relevant only in the athetoid form).
6 Family history of cerebral palsy.
7 Postnatal—meningitis.

Certain other features of the history may be helpful. There may be sucking and swallowing difficulties in the newborn period. A mother may notice that her baby feels stiff, or that one arm and leg is stiff, or that one hand is kept closed (spastic hemiplegia) when the other is open, or that the kick is asymmetrical, or that on creeping one leg trails behind.

1.   Spastic form

FIRST 3 MONTHS
The following are the principal signs:

1   A moderately or severely spastic child lies relatively immobile.
2   The hands are likely to be kept tightly closed, whereas a normal baby after 2 or 3 months keeps the hands pre-dominantly open.

53

3   The head circumference is commonly small in relation to the weight, on account of the associated mental subnormality, and for the same reason the child is commonly backward in all other aspects of development; there may be diminished alertness.

4   There is likely to be defective motor development in ventral suspension and in the prone position, with excessive head lag when he is pulled from the supine to the sitting position: but sometimes there is excessive extensor tone, so that the child seems to have good head control in ventral suspension and the prone position, but this contrasts with the excessive head lag when he is pulled to the sitting position.

5   When he is being pulled up from the supine position one may feel resistance because of spasm of the erector spinae, glutei and hamstrings; with one's hand in the popliteal space one feels the spasm of the hamstrings and notes the flexion of the knees as he is pulled up (meaning that he does not sit with the legs forward flat on the couch); and *when placed sitting forward he repeatedly falls back.*

7   The knee jerks are exaggerated and there may be a sustained ankle clonus. The plantar responses are extensor.

4 TO 8 MONTHS
The signs will be:

1   Increased muscle tone in the affected limb. Exaggerated knee jerks. Perhaps ankle clonus. Extensor plantar response.

2   A feeling of resistance when he is pulled from the supine to the sitting position, because of muscle spasm: flexion of the knees when he is pulled to the sitting position, *so that he cannot sit with the knees fully extended. When placed sitting forward he repeatedly falls back. When pulled up to the sitting position he may rise onto extended legs.*

3   Defective head control.

4   Often signs of mental subnormality and a head circumference which is small in relation to his weight.

5   In the case of hemiplegia, apart from the above, shortening of the affected limb (leg or arm—more easy to detect in the leg), and unless both limbs are warm as a result of being in a warm room, the affected limb will be cold as compared with the normal side. There may be asymmetry of movement (e.g. in kicking).

6 A spastic approach to an object. When an object such as the shining handle of a patellar hammer or a cube is offered to the child who is old enough and mature enough to reach out and get it, the spastic hand splays out in a characterstic way when reaching for it (Fig. 38).

9 TO 12 MONTHS

The signs will be the same as in the 4–8 month period. After this age, a characteristic feature of the spastic child is the development of toe walking.

2.   Athetoid form

Two factors carry a risk of athetosis—hyperbilirubinaemia in the newborn period (causing kernicterus) and severe anoxia at birth.

The signs of severe kernicterus appear between about the 6th and 10th day: the signs are stiffness, opisthotonos, rolling of the eyes, a high-pitched cry, drowsiness, food refusal, irritability and loss of the Moro reflex. There is often a characteristic posture in the lower arms, with pronation of the wrist.

After this period the signs are indefinite: they include hypertonia (but occasionally hypotonia), with delayed motor development, and perhaps a head circumference small in relation to the weight, with other signs of mental subnormality. In severe cases there may be rhythmical tongue thrusting. When the child is old enough and mature enough to reach out for objects, he will have an ataxic approach, different from the splaying out of the spastic hand.

When he is older the child with kernicterus may have difficulty in vertical gaze, enamel hypoplasia in the deciduous teeth, high tone deafness and athetoid movements: but the abnormal movements are not likely to be detected till after the 1st year.

The plantar responses in the athetoid child are flexor and the knee jerks are normal.

Snares in the diagnosis of cerebral palsy

1 Normal variations in muscle tone, briskness of tendon reflexes, motor development. All these vary considerably, and only experience can tell one what to regard as the range of normal.

2 Diagnosis of cerebral palsy on the basis of individual signs rather than on a combination of signs. One pays little attention to 1 sign, such as sustained ankle clonus in the early weeks, unless there are other signs as well (e.g. delayed motor or mental development, or a small head circumference in relation to the weight). The older the baby with ankle clonus, the more likely is it to be significant. *The diagnosis must be based only on a combination of signs.*

3 Isolated motor delay. In some families there is a pattern of later than usual sitting or walking.

4 Disappearance of abnormal physical signs. Increased muscle tone, exaggerated knee jerks and ankle clonus may disappear as the baby matures.

5 Errors in diagnosis of hypertonia. The examiner may be misled by voluntary resistance to passive movement, or by a congenital abnormality of joints which limits full movement.

6 Congenital shortening of the Achilles tendon. This causes limitation of dorsiflexion of the ankle and later toe walking: but there will be none of the other signs of cerebral palsy (e.g. extensor plantar response).

7 For toe walking, see next section.

8 Weakness of muscle due to brachial plexus injury or muscular dystrophy. The absence of signs of cerebral palsy excludes these conditions.

9 Spinal cord lesion. Weakness or spasticity of the limbs may be due to a spinal cord lesion such as diastematomyelia. If the upper limbs are normal, the possibility of a spinal lesion should be considered.

10 Degenerative diseases of the nervous system, such as Friedreich's ataxia. In the latter condition the knee jerks are absent, the plantar responses are extensor, there is pes cavus and Rombergism.

Toe walking

Toe walking may lead to a wrong diagnosis of cerebral palsy.
The causes are as follows:

Normal habit: movements of the foot are full, the plantar responses are flexor, there are no signs of cerebral palsy of the spastic type.

The spastic type of cerebral palsy.

Congenital shortening of the Achilles tendon.

Duchenne muscular dystrophy.

Peroneal muscular atrophy.

Infantile autism.

Spinal tumour.

Dystonia musculorum deformans.

The hips

Risk factors

Factors which are associated with a special risk of subluxation of the hip include the following:

Family history of dislocated hip.

Geographical factors. The condition is more common in some areas (e.g. North Italy) than others.

Breech delivery, especially with extended legs.

Sternomastoid tumour (congenital *torticollis*).

Severe hypotonia.

Spasticity.

Bilateral talipes in a girl.

Arthrogryposis.

Subluxation is diagnosed in the newborn by means of Ortolani's or Barlow's test or modifications of these. Mr. J. Sharrard FRCS was asked by me to describe Ortolani's test in readily understandable terms. He wrote as follows:

The child is laid on his back with the hip flexed to the right angle and the knees flexed. Starting with the knees together the hips are slowly abducted and if one is dislocated, somewhere in the 90 degrees arc of abduction the head of the femur slips back into the acetabulum with a visible and palpable jerk. *A mere click in the newborn period is irrelevant.*

After 4 or 5 weeks, the most important single sign of subluxation is limited abduction of the hip, with the hips flexed to a right angle. If the subluxation is unilateral, the limitation of abduction is easier to detect, because of the difference between the 2 sides. When the legs are fully extended one should note whether the internal malleoli are exactly opposite each other, for if there is subluxation there is apparent shortening of the limb so that one internal malleolus is higher. When one looks at the soles of the feet the heel on the affected side may be seen to be higher than the other.

Hips vary in the degree of abduction. The commonest causes of limited abduction of the hip are:

1   Increased muscle tone. This may be within normal limits, but if the limitation of abduction is due to spastic hemiplegia, it will be unilateral. The knee jerk will be exaggerated on the affected side, the plantar response will be extensor on that side, and there will probably be reduced dorsiflexion of the ankle on that side. If the reduced abduction of the hip is due to spastic diplegia or quadriplegia, there will be exaggerated knee jerks and extensor plantar responses are probably ankle clonus, with limited dorsiflexion of the ankle.

2   Subluxation of the hip.

3   Other hip diseases.

4   Muscle contracture—mainly when there is severe hypotonia, and when the child is constantly in 1 position.

5   Congenital shortening or tightness of the *adductor* muscle.

Note. The hip may dislocate *after* birth (and certainly does in spastic children). However many times the infant is seen, the hip must be examined each time.

Vision

Risk factors

Factors which should alert one to the possibility that the baby has a visual defect include the following:

Nystagmus.

Familial blindness.

Rubella or other infection in early pregnancy.

Severe prematurity.

Mental subnormality.

Cerebral palsy.

Hydrocephalus.

Neonatal ophthalmia.

Inspection of the eye is part of the routine examination of any baby. The newborn may keep his eyes closed, and efforts to force the eyelids open will only make him screw them up more tightly. If one swings the baby around in one's arms, he is likely to open the eyes—at least sufficiently for one to determine whether there is an obvious lens opacity.

A baby with a fixed squint seen at any time from birth should be referred to the ophthalmologist. If a squint is seen or suspected any time after the age of 6 months, the opinion of an ophthalmologist must be obtained. A rare cause of fixed squint or lens opacity is a retinoblastoma.

In the case of young infants one can determine whether there is a squint by noting the position of the light reflex on each cornea when a torch is held in front of him. The reflex in each eye should be in the centre of the pupil or at a corresponding point on the 2 corneas.

In testing an older child, one covers 1 eye with a card while one watches the other eye. When the card is slowly moved away, the eyes should not move if the eyes are straight.

Ability to follow with the eyes, and therefore, to see, is tested with the baby in the supine position by *slowly* moving the shiny handle of a patellar hammer 20–30 cm from the face, and once the baby has seen the object, from the midline to the side or the side to the midline. By 5 or 6 months, near vision is shown by the child reaching out and getting a brick, and when older, a pellet of paper. More distant vision is tested by observing the baby's interest in more distant objects or people, or by deliberately moving the shiny handle of a patellar hammer 2½ m from the baby and watching whether his eyes follow, after it has caught his attention. When in doubt (and always if there is a squint) one consults an ophthalmologist.

Nystagmus is an important condition to note, and always requires investigation.

Nystagmus is most often due to one of the following conditions:

Defect of vision (the commonest cause).

Antiepileptic drugs.

Familial.

Spasmus nutans.

Hearing

Risk factors
The following factors increase the chances that a baby may have a defect of hearing:

Deafness suspected by the parents.

Rubella in early pregnancy.

Ototoxic drugs taken during pregnancy (e.g. quinine, streptomycin, gentamicin, kanamycin, neomycin).

Familial deafness.

Prematurity, especially when extreme.

Hyperbilirubinaemia in the newborn period.

Mental subnormality.

Cerebral palsy, especially athetosis.

Neonatal meningitis.

Numerous rare syndromes.

In the first 3 months it may be difficult to satisfy oneself that the baby can hear. The sound stimulus is applied 30–45 cm from the ear, on a level with the ear and out of sight of the baby. The sounds are as follows:

PS, PHTH (both for high tones) and OOO for lower tones. One must take care not to blow into the ear.

Crinkling paper.

Squeaky toy or small hand bell.

The responses are as follows:

Startle reflex.

A cry.

Quieting if crying.

A blink.

I find that it is sometimes easier to test the baby when he is crying, when one can observe the momentary quieting.

From 3 or 4 months onwards, one tests with the same sounds, at a distance of 30–45 cm from the ear. The child turns his head to sound from 3 or 4 months. One notices in particular the rapidity with which he responds to the sound. The backward child at 6 months may respond only slowly or with difficulty. (At 7 months the normal baby turns his head to sound below the ear and a month later to sound above the ear.)

At 10 months one tests with the sound 90 cm from the ear.

When in doubt one seeks the help of an audiologist.

Action to be taken

When in slight doubt one arranges to see the child again at a suitable interval. If there is significant doubt about subluxation of the hips, a squint or deafness, cerebral palsy or mental subnormality, one should refer the child to a specialist forthwith.

One must avoid as far as possible raising any doubt in the mind of the mother until one decides that the child must be seen by a specialist. It must never be forgotten that the slightest suggestion that a child may be spastic, hydrocephalic or mentally defective will cause the gravest parental anxiety. Even the doctor's facial expression may reveal to the mother the fact that he is doubtful about features of the examination.

Further reading

DUBOWITZ V. & DUBOWITZ L. (1981) *The Neurological Assessment of the Preterm and Fullterm Newborn Infant* (Clinics in Developmental Medicine No. 79). Spastics International Medical Publications.

For a detailed discussion of development, including prenatal and postnatal factors affecting development, primitive reflexes, the assessment of maturity and other relevant facts see:

ILLINGWORTH R.S. (1980) *The Development of the Infant and Young Child, Normal and Abnormal*, 7th edn. Churchill Livingstone, Edinburgh.

For further details of hearing and vision tests see:

SHERIDAN M. D. (1958) Simple hearing tests for very young or mentally retarded children. *Br. med. J.* **ii**, 999.

SHERIDAN M. D. (1960) Vision screening of very young or handicapped children. *Br. med. J.* **ii**, 453.

Index